You Can't Change The Wind, You Can Adjust Your Sail

SHEILA NUGENT

Text Audrey Mullan
www.audreyedits.co.uk
E. info@audreyedits.co.uk

Copyright © Sheila Nugent

First print November 2022

ISBN: 9798361656899

FOREWORD

"Twenty years from now, you will be more disappointed by the things you didn't do than those you did. So, raise your anchor. Sail away from the safe harbour. Catch the wind in your sails. Explore. Dream. Discover."

Mark Twain

In this, my second book, I am throwing open my beautiful, strong sail for all to see. Etched on there is the delicate web of my life. My experiences, good and bad, forming the faint threads that entwine and weave their way across the surface.

As you read this book bear in mind that the tapestry of my life is the result of 70-years-worth of thoughts, feelings and actions. These took years to stitch together and form a fabric strong enough to withstand and sail through life's storms. Every day my sail, delicate in rest and robust in action, directs me, protects me and transports me as I travel onwards, navigating safe waters through this, at times, broken world.

My sail is unique, it is part of my identity, though I didn't always have it and I certainly did not learn to operate it overnight. I didn't hoist my sail without effort, pain or sacrifice. I was lost at sea for a long time. I was expending all my energy trying to change things that I couldn't change and failing to change the things that I could change. I was adrift.

I didn't know then what I do now, that to change your direction in life requires effort, self-awareness and lots of positive energy. In my opinion the self-healing process also requires a 'holistic' approach. There is no sense in mending the holes in your boat if there are rips in your sail. Similarly, it makes no sense to heal your body and ignore your mind. The two, I have learnt, go hand in hand.

The Soul Healer

It is not your back that hurts – it is the burdens you carry.

It is not your eyes that hurt – it is the injustice that you see.

It is not your ears that hurt – it is what you do not want to hear or hear too much.

It is not your head that hurts – it is the negative thoughts that you think.

It is not your throat that hurts – it is the words you do not say.

It is not your stomach that hurts – it is your soul not able to digest what is going on.

It is not your liver that hurts – it is the anger burning within you.

It is not your heart that hurts – it is the lack of self-love.

It is not what you eat – it is what eats at you.

Love of the self is the most powerful medicine.

Love Love Love Love Love Love Love Love Love Love yourself always & in every way.

"Health is a state of complete harmony of the body, mind and spirit."

BHS Iyengar, yoga guru

Only 20% of the healing process is mental thought, while 80% is sheer perspiration and hard work.

Through my continued teaching work in energy and reflexology I have come across many people who are 'stuck'. Drifting at sea, directionless, lying in the bowels of the boat wishing they were up on deck, charting its course.

I teach them that if they are to heal and sail into a place of self -love they need to participate in their own healing. My reflexology teaching is also holistic with personal development at its core. I take the entire body and mind into consideration, not just the feet.

In life, I strive to adopt a holistic attitude. I try to advocate for it through my thoughts, words and actions every day.

This book is for everyone. Whoever *you* are, this book is for *you!* It is not a reflexology book. It is not a therapy book. It is not a textbook nor a self-help manual. It is a frank and honest journal charting a few ups and downs in my life and sharing what helped me reach a place of self-love and acceptance. I'm not a mind reader or a healer, I am merely a facilitator who is proud to say that my work has inspired people with broken sails to rest and restore. Eventually, when the time is right, they can adjust themselves in order that they may journey in the right direction towards self-acceptance and love.

My reflexology students participate in what they learn, they apply my teaching to their own lives and transform their outlook on life. My dream is that by applying the words and exercises in this book you will do the same.

So, let me ask you: How is your sail? Tattered? Tied up? Let me help you mend it. Let me help you throw it open to the wind.

In this book I hope to gently guide you from the shore, through the changing, often choppy waves of life, to a peaceful port where you can look at your reflection in the water and love what you see.

"Health is a state of complete physical, mental and social well-being, and not merely the absence of disease or infirmity."

World Health Organisation, 1948

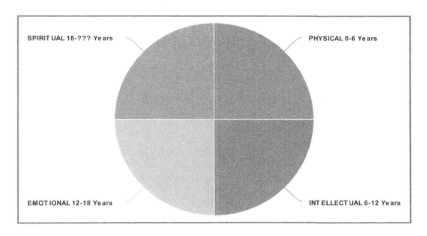

My book does not exist to teach you techniques, theories or practices in any particular therapeutic discipline. It exists merely as a resource that you can dip into, lift and open anywhere at anytime knowing you will gain strength, hope and inspiration from the pages within.

In saying that, I can only draw on *my* experiences in order to tell *my* story, so the book will feature *my* passions, *my* quirks, *my* traits, *my* issues, *my* hang-ups and *my* epiphanies.

"Show me the child till the age of 7 and I will show you the man/woman."

Aristotle

I didn't have much confidence growing up. I was a girl in a boy's world. I wasn't thin, pretty, smart or a boy. I didn't go to boarding school like my sisters, and from 13 years old I worked every hour God sent in the family business, The

Steak and Chicken in Cookstown. I was a hard worker and always gave the *impression* of being confident. I looked confident and acted confident, yet I never truly felt confident. I never felt *good enough* until I learnt through therapy that I am and always have been.

I am 70 now and a genuinely confident person. I run a hugely successful school of holistic reflexology and have taught 1000s of students over the years.

Despite being dyslexic, I have also published my autobiography 'It Won't Always be Dark at Half Past Four' which tells the story of my life. Writing it activated buried feelings that took me even further along my road of self-discovery, and it was worth it.

In this book I let down my defences, to share a little of what I have learnt so that you can apply it and come to believe that *you are enough* too.

As you work through the exercises provided and apply the advice I share, my hope is that your own story of healing will unfold.

Maybe one day you will tell your story and help others.

Believe me if I was able to get myself to a place of calm after the storm, you can too, no matter who you are.

CHAPTER ONE

"There are two things you cannot do with energy: You cannot create it and you cannot destroy it. However, you can transfer it, use it and feel it."

Albert Einstein

Before reading any further, please join me in a simple exercise to feel your own energy (or power if you like). Even if you have little or no understanding of energy. Even if you do not believe in it or call it something else (e.g., spirit, personality, vibe, aura etc.), please rub your hands vigorously together now and feel the heat this generates.

Your energy introduces you before you speak.

I believe this warmth is your unique energy. It is evidence that you are a living, breathing creature whose place in this world is just as relevant as anyone else's. This heat or energy is what you share with the world when you move, laugh, cry, feel, think or speak.

Your energy is worth more than any 'stuff' you own. Your energy is your essence in the world and the universe. The greatest gift you can give to another is your thoughts, intentions and energetic love. Use your energy today to bless the ones you love.

I believe we send our energy out into the universe and collect it again. Therefore, I believe if we send out only negative energy it will attract only negative energy and this energy will come back and impact our lives in a negative way.

What we need to do to be happy, healthy people is use our positive energy. After many years of studying, I can say with my hand on my heart that if you radiate positive energy into the world you *can* change it for the better.

I was so inspired by this discovery in my 30s, that I made it my life's work to help others change their energy, by changing their negative thought patterns and behaviours. So, 40 years on, when my students tell me that I've inspired them, it makes all my hard work worthwhile. To know someone else's quality of life has improved through my lessons is all the job satisfaction I need.

The other day Arúna was cutting my big toenail which had grown inwards (due to buried past thoughts unearthed by writing my book). I was grimacing and Christian, my four-year-old grandson, came over and pressed on my thumb and said, "Granny, the electricity (energy) will go down to your toe and make it better." What wisdom!

I asked Christian when he was four and a half, what age he was. He said, "Half past four." How ironic as this is the name of my first book 'It Won't Always Be Dark at Half Past Four'. Christian may look like, walk like, and have the love of horses his daddy Thomas has, yet he has his mother Arúna's holistic intuitiveness.

Today, as the author of two books, a wonderful new venture for me, there's a different energy building inside me and I am excited to see what impact this will have on the world.

Mummy's words are always with me.

"Reach high, don't reach low. Reach for the sky and the stars. If you always reach high you might fall to the horizon, though if you only reach for the horizon you will fall to the cold, hard ground."

Teresa Conway

Recently, when I mentioned to a friend that my first book was for sale on Amazon, they told me that Jeff Bezos, the owner of Amazon is worth billions of dollars. About a week later I read that Jeff Bezos's parents invested in his belief that he could sell books online. He started in his garage with one vision, just a solitary great idea that he worked extremely hard on. Now he is a billionaire. I thought to myself, there's a man who channelled his positive energy and reached for the sky.

He scaled great heights through hard work, sweat and I'm sure, a lot of self-doubt along the way. My vision for my books is simple. I dream that everyone who reads them will believe that they have the power within themselves to reach for the sky and achieve great things.

If you are a person of Christian faith you will know the Bible story about the three talents.

The first servant buried his talent and it died, the second squandered his and the third invested his and it grew. This story is about money which I see as energy. It illustrates perfectly how we, as people, have an invaluable energy that we can use to enhance the overall spirit of the world if we channel it wisely.

Give your unique energy back to the earth and watch it blossom.

Use this book to discover your unique light. Apply its teachings then let your newly discovered light shine as a guide for others who are struggling on their journey.

Daddy was a quiet, deep-thinking man and a wonderful philosopher. He taught me that those who don't take risks, who bury, squander or hide their energy are destined for failure. They merely exist rather than live. They put down their anchors, cling to the port and watch enviously as others set sail towards their goals. I was one of these people for too long.

Daddy was a visionary who is fondly remembered for all his wise sayings. I give great thanks for these as they have guided me throughout my life.

One became the title of my autobiography, 'It Won't Always Be Dark at Half Past Four'. In other words, life will not always be dark and difficult. Time *will* pass and the light *will* come. A new season *will* dawn. Two other favourites of Daddy's sayings were; "If you take a risk you might fail, if you don't take a risk you are sure to fail," and, "It took a man forty years to learn patience".

As a professional holistic therapist, I look back on Daddy's outlook on life and I truly believe he was a pioneer of holistic therapy.

He taught all ten of his children that we are made to manifest the wonderful power that's within *all* of us. Daddy treated everyone fairly and with mutual respect, so we got the message loud and clear, that we are no better than the next person. When I think about the power within me, even at 70, I feel a renewed energy surging and spurring me on to create even *more* great things.

> Get a piece of paper and a pen, or open the notes app on your phone, and list, straight off the top of your head, some **great things** you would like to achieve. Remember to aim high! Now, take a look at your list and note down what you **can** do to achieve them.

I came to reflexology in the 1980s when I was in my 30s. I had been running away from myself as fast as I could. By that stage I had repressed all of my life's negative feelings and experiences. I already had a full-blown inferiority complex. I'd lost a baby to Sudden Infant Death Syndrome, I'd endured crippling, recurrent Post Natal Depression, Post Natal Anxiety and Post Traumatic Stress Disorder. I was prepared to look anywhere else on earth for a solution to my empty life other than inside myself.

I flitted from one potential lifeline to another. Instead of taking time to heal and restore, I held my breath and raced to and from courses on anything and everything on a desperate mission to be OK. Unlike a confident little boat sailing boldly onwards with poise and purpose, at 30 years old I felt like a heavy, sinking, vulnerable and lost cargo ship.

It turns out my cargo was simply too heavy for me to carry alone.

Only when I chanced upon specific healing workshops (led by my *angels on earth*), and discovered yoga and reflexology along the way, did I find *my* way. With the right people by my side, and the right words soothing my broken heart, I had the courage to stop, stand still and look within. Only then did I realise that the confident, happy Sheila I had portrayed to the world was a fraud.

Standing still petrified me at first. Eventually, though, of all the places I had tried escaping to, this journey into self turned out to be the most liberating.

Life is like an egg... if it is broken from the outside its life ends. If it is broken from the inside life begins and it hatches a chick.

With a lot of help and support, and after a lot of tears, screaming and anger I recognised just how broken I was on the inside. Through years of therapy and healthy soul-searching I healed myself from the inside out. I harboured the courage to break through my cocoon and emerge as *the real me*. I am no longer a fraud. What you see is what you get, and most of the time I am happy to say, this is a peaceful, content Sheila.

In the mid 1990s I was in such a good place, emotionally, that I produced a relaxation CD called 'Moving On'. I had reached a time in my life where I felt that at last, I was content. I liked who I was and I was moving in the right direction. The CD cover design was very important to me. It was inspired by a small clay figure that I owned. A delicate little thing that was curled up in the foetal position with its head down on its chest. I asked the designer to put three images on the front cover. The first curled up, the second standing, looking at its feet and the third standing tall and looking straight ahead.

The first reminded me of all the times in my life when I did not feel enough. The second image was like me in the 1980s when I started doing every course imaginable to try to escape actually looking within myself, and the third image, the figure standing tall was when a revitalising energy shift happened within me, when I discovered reflexology and Arúna my daughter was born.

I remember when my CD cover design first came back to me all those years ago, the designer had drawn the third image with its head slightly raised and looking upwards. I asked that it be changed to look straight ahead, without any hint of superiority.

I am delighted to say that I continue to walk with my feet firmly planted on the ground, my head tilted neither upwards nor downwards and my eyes fixed directly ahead of me on the NOW.

CHAPTER TWO

Love yourself for who you are and not what other people expect you to be.

I began treating people in the 1980s when no one had even heard of reflexology let alone believed in it.

Starting out I was not confident. I was defensive of this 'strange' practice and gave long explanations of all its complicated theories to anyone who would listen. After a while I learned to accept that if others didn't believe in it that was OK. I believed enough for myself and my clients so that all they had to do was lie back, let go of their stress and reap the benefits of the therapy.

Soon, it didn't matter that people scoffed at *this rubbing of the feet nonsense*. All that mattered was that I believed in it with all my heart because I could see that not only was it transforming me as a person, I was also helping others to help themselves.

Reflexology changed *my* life. What is going to change yours? What is *your* passion? What do you believe in with all your heart? Could you share it with others? Could you pursue it in a professional capacity? Could it be the catalyst for bringing you confidence and fulfilment?

Reflexology has brought me true confidence. Today I am sure of myself. I am in no doubt that I am equal to everyone else. I am comfortable in my own skin and at ease with what I do and say.

After *treating* clients for many years, I moved into *teaching* reflexology and continue to do so with joy and passion in my heart today.

Change your thoughts, change your mind.

To self-heal, change is essential. For many, breaking the patterns of a lifetime, especially negative thought patterns can be a daunting concept, yet I believe anyone can do it if they accept help and take it step by step. Have you ever noticed the distance a baby can cover with encouragement from its parents, despite taking tiny steps? You can do the same with a support network to catch you if you fall and put you back on your feet.

In this book you will find a few simple practical exercises to help you calm your mind and let go. Participating in these can help you slowly and safely adjust your thoughts, and therefore your feelings, in order that your actions and reactions become healthier. Reading this book will not, however, keep difficult emotions at bay nor will doing every exercise make you immune to hurt, sadness or loss. What it *will* do is remind you every time you read it that you *do* have the power within you to deal with everything life throws at you. It will teach you how to live in a self-enhancing rather than a self-sabotaging way.

At the very least, this book is designed to reassure you that whatever trials you face you are never, ever alone.

> Before you begin the journey of self-discovery and healing, let me ask you to do this. Wherever you are right this minute, observe your breath. This just means be aware of how you are breathing. Feel it and listen to it. Please don't adjust it to be what you think it should be. Just let it be however it is right now. Put your hand on your chest and the other on your tummy and count the in-breaths and out-breaths. Be aware of how deep or shallow your breathing is and also where the breath is going on the inhale. Is it only going as far as your throat, your chest or right into the tummy?

For many of you, your breath will be short, shallow and much faster than it should be.

Whether you are a teenager, middle-aged or entering the twilight years, to self-heal and move on everyone needs to learn to breathe correctly. Everyone needs to be able to be still in this very chaotic world and know how to breathe freely and fully.

A healthy breath is a slow, deep and calming one. Get it right, practice it regularly and I promise it will transport you to a place of light, calm and comfort.

When I first learned how to breathe correctly I loved tapping into this new technique at every opportunity. I relished the fact I had total control over this, my body and mind's natural life-force. Changing my breath has helped me change my negative perception in life. My breath was one of the keys to finding myself. Learning and practising different breathing techniques was all part of the process that helped me turn my face inwards and find the true Sheila during the 1980s.

If you are a young person (aged anywhere between 12-30) reading this book I would urge you to take a bit of advice from an old bird like me and learn how to stop and take deep breaths.

In my opinion, young people are stuck in the fast lane. The mental health crisis and its horrific statistics among this age group are proof of this. It seems like the younger generation want everything now. They need instant gratification. The monster that is social media has its claws deep into our younger people, forcing them to strive for a perfection that isn't anything close to perfect (given the tweaking, airbrushing and filtering that goes on). Honestly, this terrifies me. The speed at which they try to live their lives will catch up with them someday when they face an inevitable burnout or breakdown. I am living proof of this.

Young people please, please, please slow down for the sake of your heart, your skin, your mind, your digestive system and your brain.

When I watch young people buried in their phones or trying to tick every box on a 'bikini body' social media checklist, I think about my daddy. I always respected him and knew his advice to us as young people was probably very wise, yet as most young people do, I ignored it and did my own thing.

When faced with a problem, Daddy would have silently, slowly and calmly sucked on his pipe and walked away to think it over. He didn't rush. He waited, he pondered and then made his move. I don't ever recall him making a foolish move. He was the wisest and smartest man I knew. I only wish I had behaved more like him when I was younger.

Even now at 70, when I feel I am in danger of behaving irrationally, putting my finger in too many pies, or trying to be all things to all people, I channel Daddy. I stop, suck in a big deep calming breath, remove myself from the chaos, ponder the situation, sleep on it and *then* act on it.

Younger readers, if you have an older person in your life that you admire, take a leaf out of their book and keep emulating them. This way, by the time you are my age you will have a lush, leafy and fertile foundation on which to raise your children wisely and well.

CHAPTER THREE

"No one's life is a smooth sail; we all come into stormy weather. Yet it's this adversity – and more specifically our resilience – that makes us strong and successful."

Tony Robbins

Now that you have mastered how to engage with your breath, take yourself to a quiet room with no distractions and get ready to nourish and explore your mind and soul.

First, a universal truth that I would like to share with you....

You create your problems and therefore only you can heal them.

Discovering this was a massive lightbulb moment for me in my self-healing journey. While it felt a little daunting at first, it was by far the most liberating thing I ever learnt.

Take a moment and read this aloud wherever you are:
"I create my thoughts, my thoughts create my feelings, my feelings create my actions and my actions result in me moving or staying stuck."

Let yourself feel empowered by the fact that you don't need to go looking for a solution to your problems anywhere other than inside yourself.

Another liberating truth that has transformed my outlook on life is: **The only person you can change is yourself.**

You cannot change anyone else's thoughts, feelings or actions, only your own.

Trust me, the energy you waste trying to change those around you is better used changing yourself. I speak from experience. As you read the following story think about someone you have tried to change. We all have one.

For years I tried to change my husband Donald by sending him on courses. He didn't change. The man just wasn't for changing no matter what I did or said. After many years of trying to change others (or hoping they would change), I finally came to the realisation that the only person I could change was myself and gradually through all my training in holistic therapy I discovered the tools to initiate change at a deep level within myself.

To self-heal you have to be very honest with yourself about yourself. This is painful and takes time, though it's worth it. It's a very sad reality that a negative mental state is a breeding ground for disease.

It's a fact that most physical health problems are exacerbated by our emotions; they start in our thoughts, then become emotions which are manifested in our physical bodies. These are what I call our 'gut feelings'.

If you are in a very dark place within your soul, with a heavy heart, because you feel like you are a negative person, with only negative thoughts, emotions, behaviours and mindset, do not despair. I have been that person and there are many more like you out there. That feeling of hopelessness you feel is like hell on earth. Blackness and bleakness all around. I also know how frustrating it is when people speak into your darkness and say things like, "You just have to focus on the positive!" or "Come on, your family needs you." or "Get up, dust yourself off and get on with it." or "Things will get better." or "Give it time. Time is a great healer." or "There is light at the end of the tunnel."

I am the first to appreciate that if you are in the darkest of places these platitudes will mean nothing to you.

When you are so low you do not feel you have the energy to breathe or blink, let alone stand or move. However, what you *do* have the energy to do is *think*.

Imagine yourself like a little seed being pushed into the ground. Way, way down into the darkness of the soil where you must stay to grow into something beautiful.

Even this little seed, packed full of all the nutrients it needs to grow tall and strong above the ground has to go into the darkest depths of the cold damp soil and wait until it flourishes. And so with you. If you are in the darkest hole imaginable with no way out, all I am going to ask you to do today is try to reach out to someone you know who will just 'be' with you. Maybe someone you have been pushing away recently? Then, if you possibly can, talk to them and describe how you honestly feel, warts and all.

Now, for a truth you may not like:

The faults we see in others are often the faults within ourselves.

I believe it is only when we are willing to use everyone as mirrors to look at ourselves, that we will see ourselves as who we truly are.

People are mirrors. What you see in others has more to do with you than them.

> How does this truth make you feel? Do you agree with it? Think about someone that has traits that really grate on you. Do you also have these traits? Or was there a time in the past when you had them? Be honest with yourself!

A good friend pointed out to me that when we are pointing the finger at someone else there are three fingers pointing back at ourselves. I found that very humbling. Whether we like it or not, how we interact with others has a huge impact on our own mental well-being and enjoyment of life.

Do you spend all your time scrutinising others, blaming them for how they make you feel, wishing they would change? I spent years doing this, so take my word for it, and I say this in love, continue to live like this and you will never love or heal *yourself*. The reality is no one can *make* you feel anything. You *choose* to feel how you feel. The sooner you grasp this, the closer you will be to self-healing.

I've always been attracted to reflexology because it links the parts of the feet to how we think, feel, create, act and move. I also adore the symbology that comes with the practice, that our soul is reflected onto our soles. Knowing and believing this is what fuels my passion for teaching this wonderful therapy. However, you do not need to be a reflexology enthusiast to understand that negativity of thought breeds negativity of body.

In order to change unhealthy thought patterns, you must first be aware of them. Taking your focus off others' lives and their faults will help you do this.

Now let's take a look at the power of our thoughts and feelings. Fill in the phrases below with the first negative word that comes to mind.

I think

I feel

I act

I create

I move

I enjoy

Hopefully you will see how one negative thought leads to another. Here's the good news, it's the same with positive thoughts. Try it.

I became aware of my self-berating tendencies as a child. Only when I learnt how to stop my negative thoughts in their tracks as an adult, was I able to change my behaviour. It took time to understand that *I* was the creator and the designer of *my* thoughts, so only *I* could change them. I had to accept that I was never going to be my bright, academic sisters or my pretty, thin friend. I was always going to be *me,* so the best thing *I* could do was focus my energies on being the best version of *myself*.

You need to take your time to do the same. Self-awareness and self-healing cannot be rushed so go easy on yourself. There are no quick fixes here.

It is not a matter of going to the doctor, therapist, reflexologist etc. and getting a prescription, great words of advice, or a specialised treatment if you are not prepared to participate in your own healing. All this will do is mask the symptoms of a deep festering emotional wound. Self-healing is a physical, mental and spiritual journey; a process that you must participate in and work at.

As I have said before, people who opt for quick fixes are often convinced that they don't have the physical energy or the mental capacity to help themselves. They feel too sad, too broken, too lost. They are convinced they need someone else to fix them. They are too frightened to look inside their own consciousness for the tools to heal.

These tools are in all of us, though until you are stronger you may need to allow yourself to be vulnerable and find that special person who can help you find these tools and teach you how to use them.

> Wherever you are now, if practical, acknowledge aloud that you feel 'stuck' and decide who you are going to share your pain with in a safe and caring environment.

Remember, baby steps add up. With the right support network, you don't need to stand until you are ready. Start by slowly and gently lifting your head up out of the darkness of your soul and locking eyes with someone who wants to help you.

I remember working with a woman who was abused by her uncle as a child. He had come back into her life as an adult and she was traumatised. She wanted to end her life as she felt she couldn't cope with it anymore. She thought she had dealt with it over the years, and now she suddenly realised she hadn't. She was living life to the full when this person came back and the memory of what he had done to her was overwhelming her.

Sometimes when I am faced with a difficult situation, words aren't always going to help, and so it was with this lady. Asking her how she felt was not going to work, she was too distressed. So I closed my eyes and I prayed that I would know the right thing to do and say.

Shortly after this I felt that 'the powers that be' were simply telling me to treat her feet as I would any other client.

I believed that reflexology could work miracles, and that day it did.

The lady didn't speak throughout her treatment. Her head remained down and she kept putting her hand over her eyes as if in shame, not wanting to look at me.

As she was leaving my treatment room, I put my hand on her arm and felt inspired to say, "If you do what you are thinking of doing, you will have to come back and do this all over again."

I didn't understand why I had said this. I knew she didn't believe in reincarnation.

In the days and weeks that followed I had to let go of the entire situation because I couldn't carry her problems into my life. I can assure you this is not easy.

I handed the situation over to my Creator because that's all I could do.

At this time in our lives, Donald and I had a holiday home in Donegal. He was working during the week and coming up on a Friday and staying until Monday morning. He would bring the post up with him and one day I saw a letter addressed to me in familiar handwriting. I was reluctant to open it at first. When I did, I looked at the signature and realised it was from this woman. It was a beautiful letter filled with gratitude. She said when she left me that day she kept thinking about how much she really didn't want to have to come back and "Do it all over again." I stood there with the restorative sound of the ocean behind me and whispered aloud, "Thank you, God, thank you, thank you, thank you." (My students will tell you I always say three thank-yous when I am super grateful.)

I was delighted that she had decided life was worth living and that she had the strength to journey onwards. She had found the people to support her to heal herself.

This lady reinforced to me that even the most broken of us *can* manage to do things when faced with adversity and difficult situations. It reminded me that there is *always* help out there, sometimes we just have to reach out and ask for it, which can be the most difficult step.

During this lady's first treatment I applied the holistic therapy approach known as *the triangle* (see diagram), an approach I use in all of my relationships, professional and personal. I would urge you to do the same.

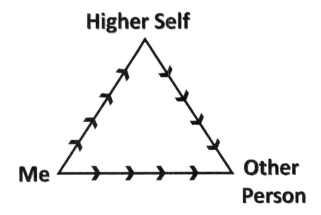

I visualise myself in the bottom left corner of the triangle, with *my* Creator at the top of the triangle (insert *your* own Creator) and the client/ friend who needs help in the right-hand corner of the triangle.

The first thing I do is send my thoughts and energy up to my Creator for guidance, to guide me first of all in what I should do and say, and then to guide my client/ friend in what they need to do to heal.

In this instance I had taken one look at the desperate broken look on my client's face and said, "Please, God, help me here." Crucially this released me from *my* ego and any thought that *I* could heal her. I was reminded that I am merely the catalyst, the person that is available, the flesh and blood who the client can see, speak to and hear. I then share whatever thoughts come into my head with the client and hope that this makes sense and motivates them towards self-healing.

I was merely supporting this lady to rise up towards becoming her higher, healthier, happier self. You will see in the diagram that the arrows go in a continuous cyclical path because, in as much as we put our energies into others, their progression results in positive energy which makes its way back to us, lifts our confidence and buoys us upwards towards our higher self.

It broke my heart that this woman had felt shame for something that was not her fault for most of her life. In my 70 years I have discovered all too often with clients that shame causes devastating destruction on the soul. Unlike guilt, which you can make amends for, shame goes into the very bowels of a person. For years this poor lady buried her shame by overeating and was morbidly obese. Her thinking was, 'If I make myself unattractive to men, they will leave me alone.'

As she continued to attend treatments, I praised her repeatedly for the courage she showed in acknowledging her trauma and its impact on her. I supported her and watched as, over time, she learnt to forgive, love and heal herself from the inside out.

Over the course of her treatment this woman eventually shared with me that for years, she had felt like she was the one in the wrong. I considered it a great privilege to listen to this lady's story and share in her pain.

I went on to work with her for a few years. By changing her thought patterns to recognise that she cannot eradicate what happened to her, or the feelings attached to it, she learnt to limit the impact it had on her well-being.

The greatest suffering for most people is the self-abuse that they inflict on themselves.

> Take a look at your internal environment. What is it like? Is it healthy and welcoming or is it spiky, uneven and dangerous? Is it full of love or shame?

Now it is time to talk about forgiveness. Forgiveness of self and of others. Perhaps you abuse yourself out of shame like this lady did? Maybe you abuse your body by overeating or under-eating, taking drugs, or alcohol, or self-harming.

Forgiveness is a gift to yourself from yourself. In order to forgive yourself you have to like yourself enough to want to feel free and happy.

If you wish to forgive someone for something they have done to you, you will also have to be prepared to love yourself enough to free your mind, and let go of the bitterness and anger that is controlling you.

While you are feeling angry and bitter with someone else, they will not be giving you or your pain a second thought. You are not hurting them by feeling hurt or living life like a frightened, wounded animal. So why do it?

Forgiveness will not mean you stop feeling angry about your abuser. It does not mean you forget, either, for deep hurts go deep into our psyche. It *will* mean you will no longer have to live cowering within the shadow of yourself.

Actively choosing forgiveness every single time the abuser or the deed enters your mind can keep your sailboat cruising closer and closer to the shores of self-acceptance.

This path to healing and the higher self cannot be rushed, so take your time and remember to breathe deeply.

The mind that is peaceful is the mind that is influenced by your higher self. Healing ourselves is our life's journey through occasionally stormy seas.

CHAPTER FOUR

You have the power within you to create great things. Use it wisely.

Another wonderful and liberating holistic exercise I wish to share with you is the *Figure of Eight* (see diagram below). This allows you to distance yourself from a negative thought, person or event. It doesn't get rid of bad people in your life or bad things that happened to you, though it can help detach you from them and move forward.

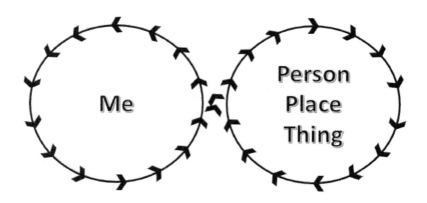

I discovered it during my training in the 1980s and it particularly appealed to me because in the field of numerology my special number is 8, which is the infinity sign on its side. Sometimes we have to go around in a circle to realise that we are back where we started. A valuable lesson can be learnt from doing all the things we think we need to do in order to discover that we didn't need to do them in the first place.

> Try this exercise with me now. Draw two circles – side by side (like the image shown) in the left circle put yourself/ me and in the right circle the person, place, thing you want to detach your energy from.
>
> You start off in the centre of the circle and think of a colour, whatever colour you want. I always imagine two golden circles. Starting at the centre between the circles, go round the right circle clockwise with whatever colour comes into your head and then anti-clockwise around the left circle of yourself. Keep going as you create the figure 8 on its side.
>
> Through visualisation/ thinking, you will start to see the person, place or thing that has been stressing you move away from you, like a balloon floating up into the sky and disappearing. Imagine that stress leaving you. If your eyes get tired just close them and continue to trace around the two circles. Do not be concerned about drawing outside the lines, just keep drawing and imagine the actual thing that is stressing you disappearing into the ether.

> Your circles may eventually merge on top of each other and move away. Again, this is good, it means you are giving your brain the message to let go.

It is advisable to do the Figure of Eight exercise to distract from stressful thoughts and avoid undue anxiety regularly. Another useful and simple exercise to calm the mind is one I call *Just Stop*.

When your thoughts are constantly negative, full of fear or anxiety simply *stop* and look at whatever is in front of you. Keep repeating what you see, no matter what it is, a brush, car, table, a pen. Then say something that makes you happy, maybe your children's names, your pet, or your favourite place to visit.

One of the most freeing facts that I discovered is that we can't have two thoughts at the same time. So, in the *Just Stop* exercise while you are repeating the same words over and over again, your mind simply can't focus on what was causing you the anxiety in the first place.

For me, who felt like I had a million thoughts in my head all at the same time, this was a game-changer. I came to accept that I was only ever thinking one thought at a time. However, they were coming at breakneck speed and my mind was close to breakdown as a result.

To combat this brain overload I began training myself to think one positive thought repeatedly (also known in the therapy world as a mantra) and discovered that doing this can stop an influx of negative thoughts in their tracks. I had a list of positive sayings pinned to a notice board in my office that my very thoughtful daughter-in-law Georgina got made into a beautiful canvas for me. They now hang in my kitchen for everyone to see. Here are three of my favourites.

Everyone at some time is going to hurt you. Make sure you choose the ones worth suffering for.

I am strong, I am confident, I am free of all suffering.

Happiness is the highest form of health.

What is your mantra? Create it now. Say it out loud and write it down somewhere where you will see it as you go about your day.

The more you can detach from negativity, the more you will reattach to your true self. To form this healthy attachment to your heart's centre you will have to make yourself and your mental health a priority.

I have met too many people, especially women and mothers, who seldom put themselves first. Please believe me when I say, unless you look after yourself properly, you won't be able to take care of anyone else.

As the saying goes, *'Love thy neighbour... as yourself!'* There is no point in running around loving and looking after everyone else if you don't look after yourself.

Looking after yourself is not a selfish thing, it's a very sensible thing, especially if you have others depending on you. For too long I took care of everyone else and put myself last. As a result I was constantly exhausted. I felt like I was nothing. I felt invisible.

In the 80s and 90s when I discovered reflexology, yoga, grief counselling and met like-minded people, I started to realise that if I didn't look after myself I would be in big trouble. I realised I couldn't share my energy if it wasn't there to give. This is when I decided I needed to make sure I always had three glasses of energy filled up and ready to go. One for myself, one for someone else if they needed it and one in reserve for myself.

I learned the hard way that if I have two glasses of energy and give one away with none in reserve, my energy will deplete and I will be useless to myself and everyone else. It's not a selfish thing, it's a sensible thing to have your three glasses full so that you can give freely and enjoy.

I am a giving person by nature. I give continuously. I love to give and I love to receive. Nowadays, as much as possible, I check to see if I have enough energy before I give any away.

CHAPTER FIVE

Fear knocked on the door. Courage answered. There was no one there.

Regardless of how good you are at breathing, being your own best friend, or stocking up on surplus energy, you cannot avoid, nor can you make yourself immune, to stress.

There is no exercise I can give you to *stop* stress entirely. Exercises such as *the figure of eight* will help you face it, use it, manage it, and emerge from it stronger and more resilient.

Stress, like fear, if managed correctly can actually be a good thing because healthy stress helps get things done.

Take a look at the *stress curve* diagram. This is a perfect illustration of how the real problems only start with stress when you go beyond its healthy stage. At the peak of a stressful situation the adrenalin's pumping and you are your most productive. Beyond this, however, lies burnout, sickness and ultimate breakdown.

The positive side is all that harmless stress that gets us up and going, gets us motivated. It keeps us at the top, at our peak, and spurred-on by positive thoughts.

It's when we go over the top of the curve that we start spiralling towards burn-out. It is vital that we do not push ourselves beyond our abilities and over the top where stress is concerned. We are not machines. Despite our brain being the greatest computer of all time, just like computers, when they overheat or deal with a virus in their system, they will malfunction if you don't address the problem quickly.

After stress comes tiredness. If we don't rest or *switch off* for a while, we are asking for trouble.

We don't need to be sleeping eight hours a night, a good 4/5 hours rest at night and a 20-minute nap in the day is ideal in my opinion. With enough restful sleep you will get things done, and you will feel motivated. If you push yourself beyond that and don't listen to the part of you that is telling you to take that two-minute pause to close your eyes, take a breath and let go, you *will* suffer mentally and physically.

Left untreated, stress can very quickly turn to disease, because when we are stressed, we disconnect from our life's purpose. We become *dis-at-ease* with ourselves if you like. When we disconnect in this way we create negativity around us, our energy dissipates and we end up exhausted. If you don't listen to that exhaustion and you keep pushing to do everything *now*, breakdown is inevitable.

Unfortunately, if you let yourself get onto the wrong side of stress you could end up at a point where stopping and lying down is no longer a choice. This is what happened when I had Post Natal Depression/ Anxiety. I went up and over the top of the curve and I fell to rock bottom because I didn't rest and restore at the peak of the curve.

Ironically, disease and illness can in some instances have a positive influence because they make you stop and reassess. They force you to ask yourself, 'What is really important in my life? Why am I running, pushing and rushing towards the grave?' Now and again, forced or not, we have to stop and take note of what is really important in life. Life goes by so quickly, it's just a flash. Time is an illusion. Trust me, regardless of what age you are you will look back and wonder, 'Where did all that time go? How can I be 30/50/70?'

Friends, the only time we are guaranteed is *NOW.*

Healthily handling stress is a continuous journey because there will always be stress in our lives. When I, or you, stop experiencing stress we will breathe our last breath.

I visualise a healthy stress-infused journey like a *spiral* where, if every wave of stress is handled healthily, you can continue to rise to the top and closer to your higher self.

I remember I was working with a person in a very low place when the image of the spiral first came to me.

I saw its mainstay, the straight line, like our backbone, the core strength we all have within us. I noticed that the spiral goes upwards as it winds around to make the next spiral. However, I also noted it has to go down slightly, then level off before it goes back up again. I decided that this reflected the ebb and flow of our lives.

When we are doing things that we enjoy and make us feel good, we are on the upwards spiral. When we get stressed the spiral goes into a dip and we come to a plateau. It is at this point that we can have a self-deprecating or self-forgiving attitude, where we can rest and restore, or become distressed and stuck. In these plateau moments, I would advise, rather than beat yourself up thinking, 'Here I am stuck again! Am I never going to learn?' decide this *is* my opportunity to learn. Do this and when you do begin your ascent again, you will rise even higher.

We all have bad days. Days when we aren't feeling great, when things aren't going right. It's inevitable that on these days we will begin to spiral downwards. Similarly, when we are feeling confident and strong, we will go upwards, gaining in strength, energy and power as we go. In these 'up moments' we are motivated, getting things done and have all our ducks in a row.

Where are you on your spiral? If you are on the plateau struggling to rise again, don't worry. We have all been there. I was there for years. I didn't need to be there for as long as I was and neither do you. However, on reflection, maybe I needed to be there for the exact amount of time that I was in order to learn from it.

Take time to conserve your energy, accept help and support, and you *will* move upwards once again.

In my life, downwards spirals have been due to illness, injury, bereavement and loss.

Through holistic therapy I trained myself to recognise that when I reach a plateau it is vital that I rest. I need to take stock and use this time to apply what I have learnt to react in a healthy way. If you do this, you will rise up and move on when the time is right, and you are strong enough to do so.

Looking back, it has actually been these times of plateau that have moulded me into a stronger more self-aware person who relishes facing up to what I need to do to move on and then doing it. Travelling upwards on that spiral after the plateau, equipped with fresh resilience, strength and power is a wonderful feeling. I long for you to feel it too.

I have endured many backslides on my spiral, sometimes feeling like I have fallen from the top to the very bottom. In these times of self-doubt and desperation I have learnt that it's all well and good to rise again if we have the strength, and health of body and mind, to do so.

I learnt this when I broke my leg and everyone was doing things for me. Having a broken leg was so frustrating for me because I'm such an independent person. Still, I knew it would eventually heal and I could return to my normal routine. I was so thankful to the others who helped me, yet it got to the stage where I knew (self-aware as I am) if I didn't manage to get my socks on myself, I was going to go out of my mind! I was impatient for the plateau of rest and healing to end. I desperately wanted to stand on my own two feet again. I learnt then that you can't speed up the healing process unless you surrender and allow others to help you. Having people to lean on was vital in my overall healing of mind and body.

I am aware that on this occasion I *only* had a broken leg. Yes, it was painful, yes, it knocked me off my feet, yet I knew it was always going to heal.

This brings me to those plateaus or downward spirals that you can't imagine ever crawling out of alive. Those people who are happily moving up their spiral when suddenly they are faced with a terminal disease, a sudden death or an awful tragedy. Moving onwards and upwards seems impossible for them. I learnt this in my 20s when I was trying to stomach a cocktail of PND, PNA and grief all at the same time. I experienced it again in my 30s when my brother and brother-in-law died by suicide. It was debilitating and I couldn't see beyond the vast flat nothingness of the plateau.

"The soul afraid of dying never learns to live"

Bette Midler, The Rose

I knew that even the fear of death, while justified, could and should be handled in a healthier way.

Death is unavoidable. It is something that is going to come to all of us. As soon as we take our first breath, we are guaranteed a last breath. It is our journey between our first and last breath that is most important. Given this fact, I feel death should be prepared for and discussed in a healthier way if we are to deal better with its sting.

I believe if everyone understood and accepted death as a part of life, we could live more freely. What is the point in living in debilitating fear of something that is going to happen, regardless of what you do or don't do?

Where possible, I challenge you to live your life fearlessly.

"Fear knocked on the door. Courage answered. There was no one there."

Martin Luther King and Victor Bullen Dr. Bach Flower Remedies.

The reality is, fear doesn't stop death, it stops life.

Similarly, worrying doesn't stop tomorrow's troubles. Worry just takes away today's peace and happiness.

Don't get me wrong, readers, I am the first to know that death and the harrowing feelings of loss and grief surrounding death are some of the toughest human emotions to navigate our way through. I am not suggesting that by diminishing the fear or stigma around death that it will make it any less painful or lonely when it happens. However, if we as communities can talk more openly about death, understand the complexity of the grieving process and accept help to get through it, it follows that the magnitude of the fears surrounding death might diminish.

There have been many things written on grief, yet there is no recipe for how a grieving person ought to act. We are all unique. Some need solitude, like the wounded animal, they want to be alone in their grief. Others need people to talk to and cry about it. When your child, parents or partner dies there is no doubt that a part of you dies with them, for you are a part of them and they are a part of you.

What we should do on our journeys of self-discovery is learn how to take a healthier approach to death, loss and grief. If we can manage this, we can help others do so too.

Life is for living, not worrying about dying. Death will happen to all of us.

I strongly believe when it comes to death in Ireland there is too much of a *stiff upper lip* mentality. People try not to cry, they bottle up their emotions and get on with it as best they can to avoid making others feel uncomfortable. To me this is ridiculous. Your heart has just broken in two. Of course you are crying. Of course you are angry. Of course you are numb. You know as well as I do that neither you nor I nor anybody else can fix this. The only thing that the grieving person wants is the person who has died, and that is something no one can give them.

The sooner people feel free to express their emotions, the better, and the healthier our society will become.

I am not afraid of my own death. I have accepted that I and everyone I love will die. This acceptance has taught me not to live in fear of it. Nor to pre-empt it or obsess over it. In fact, during Covid I refused to live in constant fear of dying. **When we are born the world rejoices and we cry, when we die we rejoice and the world cries.**

If you are reading this book and languishing in an ocean of grief, I'm sorry. What I need you to know, if you don't already, is that grief is normal and there is no time limit on it, so go easy on yourself.

You may or may not know that there are five stages of grief: Denial, Anger, Depression, Bargaining, Acceptance. I have added on a sixth which is Moving On. The first four may not come in this order. Denial is usually the stage immediately after someone dies when you can't believe they are gone. Sometimes the bereaved are so shocked they go about their normal routine as if the person is still there. I have done this many times and I now call it *going out of my body*. I believe this stage is there to cushion the grief, because if we actually felt the deep pain of the loss of our loved one, we would want to curl up and die too.

If you have experienced someone saying, 'Aren't you doing well?' a few months after your loved one has died, chances are you are still in the denial stage. I have known people, the elderly in particular, who can't handle the heartache of loss, so, a short time after the death of their loved one, they also die.

The loneliness hits them like a ton of bricks because they know they can't replace the person who's gone. Often the deeper the love you had for the person, the deeper the grief and loneliness you feel. In this instance it won't matter what anyone tries to do to help you, that deep void cannot be filled. Accepting that the person is physically gone, that you'll never again touch or feel them, seems impossible.

I remember once working with a young mother whose husband had died by suicide. She went to see her doctor because the physical pain in her heart was unbearable. Her grief was unbearable and yet she felt like she had to support her young children by not letting them see her cry. In times of grief, we *need* to let that pain out; scream and shout if it helps. Unfortunately, in our society this is still somewhat frowned upon. To avoid 'making a scene' people internalise the anguish and the physical body takes the hit by manifesting itself as depression, ulcers, cancer – the list is endless.

People often talk about the *light at the end of the tunnel* in times of sorrow. I know that when you are in the depths of grief you cannot seen the tunnel, let alone the light. I know it's not always as simple as that. It is a spiral we are navigating in this life, not a tunnel. This life has many twists and turns before we see the light at its end.   People need help and support to navigate their spiral. They don't need preached at or bombarded with clichés. They need someone next to them on the downwards sweep and throughout their plateau moments. They need hope even when their situation seems hopeless. They need to learn how to deal with the inevitable (often sickness, death or loss). They need a good crew around them when stormy waters force them to run aground.

This makes me think of Jesus in the Garden of Gethsemane when he was facing the darkest night of his soul. He needed his friends to support him, pray with him, watch with him, and they kept falling asleep. His disappointment is palpable when he asks his friend and disciple Peter: "So, could you not watch with me one hour?"

This is what we as holistic therapists, passionate teachers, and loyal friends are called to do. Be with someone in the darkest, loneliest hour of their soul. Sit with them, without judgement. Listen to them and just be with them.

This book is designed to help you get to know yourself, adjust your ways and become your own best friend. Only then can you be a good supportive friend to others. In order to do this, you need solitude. Like Jesus in the story you need to make time alone a priority if you are to get to know and improve yourself.

Unlike the terrifying territory of loneliness, aloneness is positive and empowering because it is the time *you* choose to regain your energy. As Daddy would have said, *"It's a time to recharge the batteries."*

He knew how important it was to be with your thoughts and feelings in order to understand and love yourself.

Take a few moments alone to recharge your batteries. Use this time to think about how you handle death and grief. Should you, and could you, handle it better? Do you know anyone who is grieving and languishing in loneliness? Use your aloneness to think of ways you could be there for them in their loneliness.

CHAPTER SIX

If you don't love yourself, you haven't the capacity to love others.

I understand more than anyone that there is a very real danger of these plateaus on our spiral of life becoming unhealthy comfort zones. They give *comfort* only because they *feel* safe and familiar. In reality these are spaces where we will fester, get stuck, or ill if we hang about too long.

For much of my life my comfort zone, my safe place, was going *out of my body* and hiding behind a mask of confidence.

I wore this 'face' after my own baby died, and throughout every bout of PND and PNA, when I confidently wheeled my immaculately turned out children in their beautiful pram along the main street in Cookstown. I was dying, if not already dead inside after the birth of my two eldest children. When I got home behind closed doors I was like a terrified, caged bird with broken wings. I was choosing fear over freedom, familiarity over genuine comfort.

I convinced myself that I felt safe behind the mask, even though it was a false security. What I *needed* was to be with someone I could trust to share my real thoughts with, someone who could help me help myself. Only then would I move forwards and upwards. Only then would I feel truly comforted and safe.

Sadly for me, I did not get help for many years. When I wasn't rooted by fear to a plateau, I was spiralling downwards at speed towards flatlining completely.

Luckily a wonderful doctor discovered it was my hormones that were out of balance. I would plummet down and then bounce back up and then down again – I called this my bungee jump phase. Once identified, and with the right treatment, it passed.

I would urge you, please, don't leave it as long as I did to seek help. Remember, the only time we have is NOW. Remember that false security is exactly that, false.

What is your means of escape or comfort? Eating, drugs, drink, multiple relationships? The stark reality is that the freedom or release you feel indulging in these things will be short-lived. In the long run, they *will* stifle your journey towards total health and happiness of body and mind.

So, if you take nothing else away from this book take this, **you deserve a healthy, free and happy life.**

Fear is often what keeps us spiralling, or at best, rooted to the spot in our comfort zone, indulging in bad habits or addictions.

With any fear, big or small, you can choose to stay frightened and unable to progress or you can choose to do what it takes to push through the fear and use it to become a stronger person.

Whatever the source of your fear; loss, death, loneliness, the unknown, change, the *feeling* of fear does not need to consume you.

Remember: **change your thoughts, change your feelings. This will change your life!**

Our home is in our mind, so please, be as comfortable as you can in your home.

With enough support from others and an increased self-awareness you can choose to overcome most fears and anxieties.

A little bit like stress, fear can be channelled in a positive way. Sometimes, to discover just how strong we are, it is good to face the fear and do it anyway. Do this and you might even discover that outside your comfort zone is a wonderful place for you.

Let me explain how I discovered this in my life.

My sister Anne was very clever and went to America in early 1970. I had dyslexia and was not academic like her. I was in awe of her and used to try to write her meticulously spelled and grammatically correct letters every month (there was no WhatsApp then and it cost a fortune to telephone). Anne was always a great speller, so when I was writing to her, I really struggled to get it exactly right. I used to have the dictionary to hand to spell the words correctly! That's how deep my feelings of inadequacy were about my academic ability back then. And yet I wasn't stupid, I was dyslexic.

When I started teaching reflexology my good friend and partner-in-crime Phyllida used to write on the flip chart and spell for me. So, when she moved on to work with Elisabeth Kübler-Ross it was panic stations! Suddenly, Little-Miss-Dyslexic had no multi-degree-wielding Phyllida to spell for me. At first I avoided writing on the flip chart in class. I made sure I had all of my teaching material on overhead slides. The more classes I taught, however, the more confident I became, and one day I stood at the front of the class and said, "There are some things I am not good at and one of them is spelling. I'm sure there are some of you who are good spellers, so you can help me out when I can't spell a word."

The lesson here is, face your fears. Own the fact you can't do something. Stop being frightened of doing it and avoiding it all the time. Either admit that you struggle with it and continue doing it as best you can or stop doing it completely and find someone else to do it for you. If you can find someone to help this frees you to pour all that energy into something that you are wonderful at. This realisation took an enormous weight off my shoulders and to this day I still ask my students to spell for me, or I just write it as it comes to into my head. There is no fear in the equation whatsoever. Ironically, I now know, if my beautiful sister Anne was alive today she would say, "Sheila, don't sweat the small stuff."

Thank goodness I am not stuck in that inferior fearful mindset anymore. I know the multitude of things I *am* great at and have accepted that spelling is never going to be one of them.

> Take a moment to think about what you are not good at. What fills you with fear at the thought of it? Maths? DIY? Public Speaking? Hosting? Cooking? Is it time you stopped trying so hard? Is it time to stop covering-up the fact that you simply can't do something? Is there a way around it? Is there someone who can help you with it? Face the fear of admitting your limits then use that lovely energy you had been wasting to catapult you towards resounding success in something else.
>
> I would encourage you to allow yourself to be vulnerable, admit your fears and put your energy into something new today. There is a purpose for everyone, find yours.

And even if you try something new and are completely rubbish at it, if you enjoy it on any level, stick with it. Just because you are not good at something doesn't mean you can't get a buzz from it. I discovered this when skiing for the first time.

When I was frightened of skiing, I faced my fear and did it anyway. My inkling was right, I was pretty rubbish at it.

Still, the negative fear I felt before trying it very quickly turned to exhilaration once I was in the throws of it. I was rubbish at it, yet I did enjoy it.

Exhilaration is now one of my very favourite feelings. Even at 70 I can't get enough of it.

My first time skiing, my sister-in-law took us all to a black slope by mistake. Well, if anyone has been skiing they will know the black slope is the most dangerous, next the red, then the blue and then the (beginners) green one that I had been on. So there I was at the top of this almighty slope with only clouds below me with a choice to make. Either I fell down, rolled down or skied down the mountain.

In the end I did a combination of all three, with Anne and her friends guiding me as best they could to safety. I had a few cuts and bruises to show for it, though no broken bones, when we arrived at the blue slopes. I was so glad to see the outline of the village where there had only been clouds before. Anne and her friends still needed to burn off some energy, so once they knew we were safe, they got into a hunker position and went like rockets down the mountain. I futtered down a bit more and then thought, "Just go for it!" There was a straight bit, with nothing in front of me and the width of a football pitch on either side. So I did what the professional skiers did and got into the hunker position. Well,... off I shot and, HOLY... malony! Within seconds the adrenalin/ fear pumping in my body turned to exhilaration and I felt euphoric.

Another very natural negative feeling that could easily have stopped me trying this new and wonderful activity was jealousy. That crippling feeling which attacks every single one of us. Jealousy could easily have ruined my entire skiing experience up that mountain. I could have thought, 'Well it's OK for Anne, she's good at this. I'm rubbish at it. Poor me. I'm not as fit, as thin, as brave as the rest of them so I will just sit here at the bottom of the mountain and have myself a pity party.'

All I can say is, it would have been absolutely tragic had I missed out on that fantastically exhilarating experience.

Don't miss out on the feel-good factor because of jealousy. If this emotion is holding you back from 'having a go' in life, my advice is this: instead of being jealous of someone, put your energy into emulating/ copying them.

I remember when I was about 17 and a beautiful woman came into The Steak and Chicken. She had nails painted pink and a fabulous diamond ring. I thought, 'I would love to have nails like hers and a diamond ring.'

I have both of these now.

I didn't let jealousy consume me and root me to the spot. I thought, I'd like to have those things so I worked towards getting them.

Thought is the first process of action.

Jealousy is something within yourself. It's in *your* mind. So, the good news is you can control it. What you cannot control is jealousy in someone else. If someone is jealous of you, the problem is theirs not yours. The problem is only yours if you take it on. You cannot change anyone's mind; you can only adjust your own sail. You can only look at how you are allowing *their* jealousy to affect *you*.

People who are jealous want everything and they don't want you to have anything. They stick their noses into everyone's business and they don't want anyone knowing theirs. The reality is, we all live in a glass bowl and whether you think you are on the inside looking out or the outside looking in, everyone can see you. There is no escaping the eyes of others.

My friends, regardless of how much self-healing work you do or how lovely a person you think you are, there will always be people who don't like you. Remember, like jealousy in others, you cannot change their opinion of you. You can only change your reaction to it.

As a therapist and a person who loves and accepts myself, faults and all, I despair that people waste energy on being jealous of others. If you are one of these people, do yourself a huge favour and stop this today. Emulate instead.

I have met thousands of people in my time, and while I love to meet new people and make new friends, my priorities after myself are my family, my friends and my colleagues.

I ensure I do not try to be all things to all people anymore and I certainly don't look for a stranger's reassurance or approval. I no longer waste energy on things or people that could be better used having fun with the people I love.

I suppose you could say I have arrived at that wonderful stage of life where I don't care what others think of me.

Honestly, if I felt that it would be good for me to play hopscotch with my grandson outside I would do it. I would encourage you to do whatever is good for you, something that would boost your energy and give you a laugh.

It's so important to laugh every day, to indulge yourself in joy, laughter and fun at every opportunity. Have the 'craic,' as we say in Ireland. If you keep your energy levels topped up by having fun as often as you can, when times get tough you will have your three cups to deal with the situation.

> In order to identify **your** people, try this exercise. Imagine you were given only six months to live. Now think about how you would like to spend this time. Think about what and who you would fill your time with. You will discover by doing this what and who is really important in your life, and what and who you should be prioritising **now** in order to lead a happy, full life in the future.

We are all in this thing called life together so the way I see it, we might as well try to get along. Where possible, have a sense of humour and see the funny side of situations and people. Humans are indeed a rare breed, though remember, rare also means precious and unique.

As a holistic therapist I firmly believe in a *collective consciousness (energy)*. As humans we are constantly picking up on each other's thoughts and energy. You cannot avoid this, so I suggest you embrace it and use it wisely. Allowing yourself to absorb good people's positive energy will recharge your own energy and enhance your impact on society.

I have discovered in my 70 years on this planet that arrogant people do not use energy wisely. They suck the energy out of others and abuse it to build themselves up. Then when they think they have made it, they sit up on their high horse and are critical of others.

So, a little word for those on their high horse. The higher your horse, the further you will fall when real life hits (and it will, no matter who you are!).

In my own life when I suspect someone is jealous of me, I just feel sad that they don't love themselves enough. That they don't think they are enough. Whether it's my hair, my house, my job that they think they want, my advice is the same, *don't envy me, emulate me*. If it's my hair you're jealous of, just ask me, 'Who does your hair Sheila?' I will answer you (it's Wanda at *Wanda's* in Cookstown) and chances are I will compliment you in return. So, it's a win-win situation.

If you are a jealous person you need to believe in yourself. Hopefully this book is already helping you to do that.

From now on, instead of pulling someone down to make you feel better (it won't), try raising them up by saying, "Well done you! Look what you have done with your life. Maybe I could do similar!"

In other words, don't be the caterpillar from my first book 'It Won't Always Be Dark at Half Past Four,' crawling along, scraping the surface of the earth always looking downwards.

Look up, observe life from your own unique perspective, believing that the day will come when you will fly high as a butterfly.

Reflexology gave me *my* new life-enhancing perspective. It taught me to focus on my own healing while guiding others towards theirs. It also taught me to let go of my *fixer* mentality of old and to accept that I can only lead people to the pool of self-acceptance and love, I can't make them drink. Although I am still a controller, I am no longer a control freak. I realised there needs to be people who lead. I am a natural leader. It's OK not to be a leader, however, because when decisions need to be made, some struggle.

That's OK if you learn from the experience. Knowing when you have chosen the wrong path is a strength, not a failure. It takes real courage to admit you made a wrong decision.

Reflexology was good for *me*. I urge you once again, find what is good for *you*. Try out new things. Learn new skills. Meet new people.

When you find what floats your boat, even if it scares you, I challenge you to face your fears and do it anyway. Leap into the uncharted, cool, refreshing waters of self-awareness and enjoy a good splash about.

In my class one day I asked the students who they would like to emulate/ be like? A student said, "I would like to be like you Sheila." I was too embarrassed and shocked to say much in response. Years later, on reflection, I liked and loved myself enough to accept this as a huge compliment. I was now in a place where I could acknowledge that I *had* done great things. I *had* risen up like a phoenix from the depths of fear and negativity to shine my light and inspire others.

I needed the message of my life's work to be clear, 'We are, each and every one of us, *equal*. I AM ENOUGH and so are you.' I wanted to heal myself so that I could help others heal themselves. So even though I did rise like a phoenix and am very proud of it, I knew my place was back down on earth where I could help others rise. I have lived long enough to know that regardless of how successful or important we think we are, life does not bypass anyone when it comes to dishing out hard times.

No one is immune to getting knocked back down to earth by the realities of life, so don't let your successes go to your head. If you manage to rise out of your dark place (and I really hope you do), don't stay up there with your head in the clouds, all wrapped up in your own self-importance. You need to be prepared for the next reality check by having your feet firmly planted on the cold, hard ground with a support network around you. You are no more invincible than the next person. Life will throw you a curveball that you will not be able to handle sitting alone on top of your high horse.

Imagine you are a strong oak tree with its roots going deep into the earth. They ground you; make you strong and confident enough to face being rocked by any storm.

CHAPTER SEVEN

"A ship in harbour is safe, however, that is not what ships are built for."

Albert Einstein

I have stressed throughout this book that therapists, family, friends, and community are life-enhancing people to have in our lives. However, I cannot stress enough how vitally important it is that we also like and love our only constant companion in this life, ourselves.

The only person you have to spend all your time with and can never escape from, is you. If this scares the life out of you, you are in good company. It scared me too, yet I soon realised if I was to get the most out of *my* life I had to learn to heal, like and love myself.

I was inspired to do this by many wonderful individuals, though for the sake of this book let me mention just two of my heroes. Nelson Mandela, who emerged from solitary confinement with only love in his heart, and Dr Robie, my yoga instructor, who was paralysed from the neck down for a few years after a horrific accident.

Had Nelson Mandela let others treatment of him turn him into a bitter and angry person, his body and his mind would have been damaged beyond repair. Chances are, his negative mindset would have wreaked havoc on the body and mind of the only companion he had in prison, himself. We can choose to be a prisoner in our minds or choose freedom. Nelson Mandela choose to be free in his mind.

I can only presume that Nelson Mandela made a choice to actively change negative thought patterns while he was imprisoned on Robben Island. With so much time alone, he must have trained his brain to think positively.

Similarly, with Dr Robie. Lying there, unable to move the body he had spent years moulding into wonderful yoga poses. He had to make the choice to work on harvesting healthy thoughts in his mind so that he would emerge once again, strong in body and mind.

The language we use and the conversations we have with ourselves can have a detrimental effect on our health.

Let me illustrate this.

Think about something that is preying on your mind at the moment. Perhaps a work challenge, a difficult relationship, a looming deadline. Now make a list like the one below, think about your situation, and complete the list by writing down the first negative thought that comes into your head. Once you have done this, convert your negative words to positive ones.

Now read aloud the negative phrases and note how you feel afterwards. Has your heart-rate increased at all? What is your breathing doing?

Then say the list of positive phrases aloud. Do your feelings differ? Is your heart-rate calmer? Is your breathing deeper and slower?

Positive Words	Negative Words
I can	I can't
I am	I'm not
I will	I won't
I have	I haven't
I love	I hate
I enjoy	But
I create	I destroy
I choose	I have no choice

There are so many negative words we use daily like; BUT, probably, almost, perhaps, never, however, I need, I want, I might, I wish, the list goes on!

Add your own negative sayings to the list. Write them down and every time you say a new one write it down too. Revisit this list regularly converting the negative phrase to the positive version.

You, like Nelson Mandela, can choose to program how you think with either positive or negative thoughts. The choice is yours.

Will you choose to be a prisoner in your mind, or free?

For Nelson Mandela, although physically imprisoned for 27 years, he managed to remain free in his mind.

I can't reinforce this enough… it is *you* who thinks your thoughts, it is *you* that can change them. Your real home is your mind, we live in our minds.

Change your thoughts, change your life.

It's unlikely that any of you will have experienced physical imprisonment, paralysis or indeed a solitary life such as Dr Robie or Nelson Mandela, however, we have all faced situations in life where we, justifiably, feel like an innocent victim of circumstance or another's cruel behaviour.

If we do not work on changing our reactions to the traumas that befall us we are in danger of becoming prisoners in our own bitter, angry vengeful minds. This type of mind has very little space for love or growth.

Continuing to think of these two heroic men, trapped, makes me appreciate just how much freedom we actually have in this world. Do we appreciate this freedom enough? I suspect not.

Sometimes, without even meaning to, we become prisoners of our default tunnel-vision mentality. As creatures of habit we tragically fail to broaden our horizons beyond our street, our town or the nearest supermarket or coffee shop.

Readers, can I remind you, there's a wonderful and fascinating world out there. I would encourage you to exercise the freedom you have to explore it.

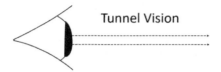

I discovered that travel was one of the best ways to make the transition from a restrictive tunnel vision to a liberating peripheral vision of the world.

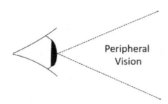

Travel does not have to mean to far-flung lands. Just one trip on an aeroplane would suffice. One experience of gazing out the window at the clouds beneath, then appreciating the jigsaw that is the land followed by the strangely comforting image of us humans, the miniscule entities scurrying across the surface of the earth.

"To reach a port we must sail. Sail, not tie at anchor. Sail, not drift."

Franklin D Roosevelt

With travel you will discover just how small a place the world really is and just how much all the busy little creatures called humans have in common.

In the course of my life, I've had the privilege of travelling the world, though my first memories of travel are going to Portstewart on the North Coast of Ireland, just an hour's drive from home.

I was about five and I remember we were in a terraced house on a steep hill (probably the hill wasn't that steep, yet to me at five years old it was). My next memory was Daddy taking us to The Battery, Ardboe where I learnt to swim. We went to Portstewart every year in our big Vauxhall PZ96. That number is etched on my brain. It was dark green and the front seat was one big bench seat. The dashboard was mahogany and at least seven of us piled in, going to The Port with our buckets and spades. It was always Daddy and his friend Billy Menary who took us. I think Mummy was glad to stay at home, as she would say: 'To get her head shired'. Billy had a pin in the lapel of his jacket which he used to take the cockles out of their shells with. He

73

always asked if we wanted one, insisting they were delicious. I thought they were disgusting.

My next big trip was a bit further away, to Salthill in Galway in 1969, at the height of the Troubles, with my boyfriend. He was a Protestant and I was a Catholic though this didn't matter to us. I met him at a dance in Loughrey College where he was studying.

We met two Danish people called Gunther and Margit in Salthill. I went to Denmark the following year to visit them. When I was in the airport waiting on my flight with my handbag beside me, I went to get a cup of tea (I didn't drink alcohol then) and my purse was stolen with all my holiday money in it. I found a phone box (no mobiles then) and phoned Daddy in floods of tears. Daddy said, 'Don't worry I will go to the bank now and get money sent to you.' I was lucky I was staying with Gunther and Margit as they loaned me enough to keep me going until the money from Daddy arrived. They were such lovely people. I remember them having a party for me with their families. I couldn't speak Danish and most of them couldn't speak English. This was the first time I experienced eating a ten-course meal. By the fifth course I was full, because I'd taken too much of the early courses (typical me the Irish gulpin!). In my future travels, which were many, I learnt to ask how many courses we were having.

In 1973 Anne and I travelled to Corfu in Greece and in 1974 we travelled to Yugoslavia and Venice. I loved Venice, especially St Mark's Square. The gondolas and the Italian food was delicious.

I got married in 1975 and we went to Tenerife for our honeymoon. Donald had dreamt of going there though he didn't even know where it was. I went to the travel agent and booked it.

Over the course of our marriage we travelled to many different places. One of my most memorable holidays during our marriage, however, was back on home soil, camping in Donegal. I remember as I was packing, our au pair Agnès said to me, 'Maybe you should take some egg cups as you have everything else apart from the kitchen sink!'

I had even taken a blow-up bed to sleep on while everyone else slept in sleeping bags on the ground. On our first night it rained. A lot! The next morning at the scrake of dawn everyone was soaked through except me. We were meant to stay another couple of nights, yet, needless to say, everything was swiftly gathered up and fired into the boot of the car, tent and all. That was our first and last time camping. When we went to a campsite in the South of France a few years later we stayed in a mobile home. What can I say? I love my comforts. No more tents for me.

The memories from all my travels bring me great joy to this day. Every place was wonderful and broadened my mind a little bit more. I have encouraged my children to travel as much as possible. If you are a parent I would encourage you to do the same with your children. I didn't want my children to have small minds when they grew up and they certainly haven't, given that my eldest daughter Lara has just moved from Dubai to New York on her own.

While immersing myself in different cultures during my travels I always managed to find common ground, even when I didn't speak the language. In Thailand, for example, they didn't need language to communicate. The softness of their energy was enough for me to understand them, and to feel close and totally safe with them.

The different faiths in other places were also strangely comforting to me because I know how comforting a personal faith can be. When Mummy and I went to Egypt in 1989, like all tourists, we went around the famous sights and tombs. I remember saying to one of the guides, "Why are there so many gods?" The guide told us they believed in a Triad and immediately I understood because in my Christian upbringing there was the Trinity, (when I was a child I used to think of these three Gods like a three-headed monster!).

Nowadays, I don't align myself with any specific religion. I see this Trinity as our three personalities in one – the father, always forgiving, the son, loving unconditionally, and the Holy Spirit, that lives and dwells in all of us. These strands are not just in some of us, they are in all of us. We all have the same power within us. It is this power I have been urging you to tap into.

While I love to travel, home is and always will be Ireland, and more specifically, Cookstown and Donegal. At one stage we were considering moving to Australia. We travelled extensively in 1989, checking out different areas, though I realised very quickly that it would never be home for me.

I love the parochial and the sense of community of home. I also love to experience the expanse of the world and different cultures. I like to have the best of both worlds. Truthfully, I discovered a long time ago that home is not a building or place. Home is in your heart and mind wherever you are in the world.

Freedom starts in your mind. Free yourself of your negative thoughts. No one else can live in your mind unless you invite them in. How you think is how you feel.

I'll say it again, "WE LIVE IN OUR MINDS."

While I would urge you to travel, meet new people and delight in your similarities, it is also vital to celebrate your differences. If we are to tap into and love our true selves, we need to recognise and celebrate our unique traits and behaviour.

Before we start celebrating them, however, we need to identify whether they are unhealthy, irrational and destructive or calm, loving and productive. If they are the former we must work on changing them. If the latter, we must celebrate and nurture them.

CHAPTER EIGHT

"We must free ourselves of the hope that the sea will ever rest. We must learn to sail in high winds."

Aristotle Onassis

Regardless of who you are, or where you live in the world, what faith you practice or how famous or rich you are, you will display behaviour learned from your family of origin. Genes, good and bad, will always be passed on in families. Healthy and unhealthy behaviours of parents will be unconsciously copied.

Early into my journey of holistic healing I learnt the importance of researching my family of origin. Doing so benefited me hugely in the self-healing process. I would urge you to do the same.

There may be something about yourself that you don't like, something you suspect you have inherited through your genes. I, for example, look like my mummy, speak like her and act like her in many ways. So much so, I am known to regularly announce to my family around me, 'I know, I know, I'm channelling Teresa.'

Thankfully, Mummy had many wonderful traits that I'm delighted to have inherited. However, she wasn't perfect and I can see where I think she went wrong in her life. I now make a concerted effort not to emulate her unhealthy traits and behaviours in my own life.

Mummy was the hardest working woman I knew. She was also the most loving and giving. Her children were the lights of her life and we very much felt that. Even with parenting she was very logical and practical. If one of us got sick she put six of us in the big double bed; three of us at the top and three of us at the bottom of the bed, in the hope the rest of us would get the bug too, to get it over and done with. She couldn't have coped otherwise and that makes sense to me.

She had ten children in a row and a business to run. She kept going even though I'm sure there were times when she was absolutely exhausted. One baby after another, getting up to feed one while another is sick, and also having to go to work. I am in awe of all the hard work the people of that generation did. They had great resilience. And yet, I often wonder just how much their mental health suffered for it.

I look back and I wish Mummy had let herself be a bit more vulnerable and rested more. I have learnt in my own life if I don't do this I burn out. For years I came across as nothing more than a hard taskmaster to others because I simply never stopped working (a bit like Mummy). I am glad I realised I was so much more than a hard worker. I am relieved that I reached the point where I didn't want to be treated like a machine anymore.

Like Mummy, for most of my life I didn't let people see my vulnerability. I was always strong Shelia; hard-working, focussed, determined, and resilient. I *was* a hard task master when I worked in our family business. I remember when Mummy came in one evening, Ann, a lady who worked for us said, "Oh don't go near Sheila, she's on her bike tonight!" What can I say? I had a strong work ethic. I wanted the workers to have the same. I wanted them to do what I was doing, which was anything that needed done. I always cleaned up my own mess and I expected my colleagues to do the same, not to cut corners or be lazy.

Tragically, away from work, I was like a tortoise hiding inside my hard shell never letting anyone see the deep feelings of inadequacy and the relentless suffering and pain. I don't know that Mummy *ever* showed the inside of her shell during her time on earth.

Mummy was undoubtedly a strong, determined sailboat who adjusted her sail every which way to protect and navigate us through life. However, no one ever got to see the intricate pattern on that sail which I have no doubt would have been battered, ripped and repaired often.

Both of my parents were wonderful influences on my life. Daddy was such a quiet, modest, wise philosopher, who always said beautiful things like, "I'm in business to do myself good, not to do anyone else any harm." However, one parenting approach they had which I did not adopt with my own family was their preferential treatment of the males in our household.

The boys in my family were treated vastly differently to us girls. We served our brothers their meals, we cooked their food, we washed their dishes. We cleaned their rooms. They did not have domestic chores dealt to them. They had honours bestowed upon them, the main one being to carry on the business in the family name.

When I became a mother, I was determined that my son Shea was not going to get any privileges over his sisters and I stuck to my word. When my son left to go to university in his wee Clio packed to the straps, he went equipped with many life skills. He went to Manchester and was living on the 10th floor of the halls of residence. He had to carry his stuff up all by himself. He also discovered he was the only one of all his flatmates that could cook.

Shea had loved to cook from no age. He was baking Christmas cakes when he was 10. I wanted all of my children to be confident and competent, regardless of their gender. Unlike the home I grew up in, my children had a linen basket outside their bedrooms and when they had a shower they were expected to clean up after themselves. The way I see it is, I didn't give my children rules, I gave them values.

Two other major influences from my family of origin that did me more harm than good were religious traditions and the endless guilt that came hand in hand with them. I had a first-class honours degree in guilt.

In my 20s I was still going to Lough Derg, a Catholic retreat to do penance and get right with God. I didn't feel like a good person, despite being there for the seventh time in my life to repent for my sins. During my stay I would be expected to walk barefoot on stones, fast, get by on very little sleep, pray and cleanse.

I remember when I was 28, standing waiting for the boat to embark on this pilgrimage. Shea, my first born, was just three months old and I was struggling with PND, anxiety and guilt. I was out of my body trying to find a way to escape myself. I didn't even know I was depressed. I realise now this retreat was just another excuse to beat myself up, something I was already very good at. I was living my life with tunnel vision, hemmed in by my family, my faith, my town, my work, my guilt.

After the seventh trip I thought, 'What is this about? What am I doing? I'm just doing what other people want me to do. I'm doing this out of guilt.'

I was acutely aware that I was a mother now. I had a little boy to influence and I knew I didn't want him at age seven to go sit in a confession box and make up sins like I had to do.

I felt like there were still religious shackles round my ankles although I knew I was ready to throw these, the veils, the indoctrinations and the conditioning, off. I was ready to be free.

I didn't go to Lough Derg after the seventh time. This marked the beginning of the end of my religious experiences. As I stood on the jetty waiting for the boat to take us off the island, I made a solemn promise to myself never to beat myself up like that again. I never went back, although now, over forty years later, I look at it differently. I now see Lough Derg as a place of contemplation and meditation, what we now call mindfulness. You never know, I might even go there again.

I desperately needed to break free from the restraints of Irish Catholic religion and culture. One fateful day I found the courage to do just that. I changed my course, adjusted my sail, and went in a different direction. I sailed into open seas, adjusting my sail accordingly. I have never looked back.

For years people thought I would take up another religion, though by now religion was within me. I continue to believe that heaven and earth are states of mind, not actual places. I see God as the Sun and we are the rays of the sun. We are all still part of the one and everyone is connected, good, bad or indifferent.

Today, I am free. I meet people who have different religious faiths and I can appreciate it's a wonderful thing for them. However, I have no time for hypocrites who dress up to the nines, go to church on a Sunday just to be seen and the rest of the week are running everyone else down. They may be going through the motions on their knees, at church, mass and confessions 24/7, yet I firmly believe it's their treatment of others that is the most important thing.

Spirituality, I believe, is how you interpret God's word and what you choose to do with it. People will do what you do, if you lead by example. When they see that you are happy and joyful and content, rather than running around with a sackcloth feeling that you have to beat yourself up all the time, they will want to emulate you.

I have been involved in a lot of charity work over the years which brought me into the company of so-called Christians. On one occasion we visited people who had come out of a mental institution to be introduced back into the community. It was not the cleanest place, and yet these women had made us a cup of tea and given us a wedge of fruit cake with big lump of butter on it. I ate the cake and drank the tea with gratitude. One *Christian* lady I was with could only see the dirt and the germs around us and refused the tea and cake. I saw the purity of the gesture and their hospitality. They made the food with love, so I ate it with love. It's as simple as that for me. I believe Jesus or any other prophet would have done the same.

I give thanks to this day at every mealtime for the hands that made the food. I give thanks that I'm fit to eat it and have the health to enjoy it.

So, friends, take a trip down memory lane right now, note the areas you wish to emulate from your own family of origin and those you do not. If you are already channelling unhealthy traits from your mother, father, grandmother, aunt, take heart – acknowledging these is the hardest part. Having identified where they come from, with your newfound holistic therapy knowledge, you can move towards changing them and have a healthier home environment for your own family.

In as much as we need to explore our family of origin, we also need to think about what sort of family of origin we are creating for our children. We can make adjustments now to ensure that our children don't transition into adulthood damaged by archaic traditions or with their parents or grandparents' bad habits in tow.

Take food and exercise, for example. Your diet and your routine will influence your child's attitude to both, whether you want to admit it or not.

In my case, I went to the other extreme with my children, which wasn't healthy either. Lets just say this was over forty years ago when organic was a strange word. I only let them eat healthy, organic food; no chocolate, no fast-food, no sugary snacks. In their lunch-boxes were celery sticks, carrots and fruit until one day I was cleaning Shea's bedroom and behind the dressing table I discovered chocolate bar wrappers hidden away. I asked him about them and he told me he had swapped his fruit and veg for a boy's chocolate bar because the little boy had never tasted an orange. My best friend Geraldine asked me if I was going to get Shea a birthday cake when he was one. I got him one and he was sick as a dog after eating it. This just reinforced the importance of balance, balance, balance as a parent.

I wonder if we as parents ever get the balance right? We can only do the best we can with what we have, though let me remind you, 'Show me the child to the age of seven and I'll show you the woman or man.'

After many years of beating myself up about my weight, my diet and my body shape, I finally reached the belief that the best approach is a balanced one. Today I live by the refreshing notion that I can eat what I like as long as it's in moderation. There should be a balance in your relationship with food. You should enjoy it, just don't overdo it. When my students are going home for Easter, I always tell them, "Enjoy every last second of your Easter eggs!" If eating something causes only guilt and self-loathing, don't eat it. We live in our minds so if you think the Easter egg is bad for you, then it is.

Children need to be educated about healthy choices and if this isn't done at home, it ought to be taught in school, because school has a big influence on children. Hopefully you are in a position to teach your children by example, because I truly believe that like so many skills, this should be taught young. Think back to your own childhood, what life skills do you wish you were taught?

Even if a child is unlikely to see a vegetable from one week to the next, at least if healthy eating and a healthy mind is taught in schools, the seed is planted. When they are older the hope is that that seed will have grown and they can make the healthy choices that were denied to them by parents growing up.

In as much as we all have our own relationship with food, so too with exercise. Exercise is a very personal thing. All too often we fall into the trap of doing what everyone else is doing because, "If it's good enough for them, it's good enough for me." Sadly, it really doesn't work like that as I discovered the hard way. You have to find what *you* enjoy if you are going to stick with it and see results. I finally see, at 70, that there was no point in me going to the gym, pumping iron or running on a treadmill for all those years. I didn't enjoy one second of it and yet I stuck with it and even had a personal trainer three mornings a week. She used to say, "You'll get the buzz, Sheila! Keep going and you will get the buzz!" I *never* got the buzz. I came away exhausted. So, eventually through holistic therapy I tried to treat exercise as something in my life to be enjoyed.

I suggest you do this too. Whether it be walking, cycling, running or swimming, do what makes you happy.

Take a moment to think what that might be for you. Are there classes in your area? Could you teach it? Can you think of other people that might enjoy it?

I am a water-person. I've always loved swimming. Years ago, when I was very fit I used to go to the pool and swim a mile, three mornings a week with my dear friends Debbie and Hilda. Back then I often passed an aqua-aerobics class and scoffed at all the 'old' people thinking they were exercising. Well, I've reached that stage now where I *am* the old person and I love aqua-aerobics. Believe me, it can make you as fit as a fiddle if you want it to. I go three mornings a week and Carly puts us through our paces on Tuesday and Thursday morning. There's certainly no slacking off. It's brilliant.

Then there's Rosie's class on a Wednesday morning. I call us Rosie's Dancers. We dance up and down the pool doing our seven steps, or the Riverdance, as we call it. We do the waltz and the cha-cha-cha. I always joke that all we need are castanets to do some Mexican dancing. It's great fun and you come out knowing you have done a great work-out for the body and the mind.

CHAPTER NINE

"A smooth sea never made a skilled sailor."

Franklin D Roosevelt

Wherever you are on your journey to a healthy body and mind if you are struggling with an addiction chances are your sailboat is either stuck in the port or drifting directionless at sea. If this strikes a nerve for you, don't worry and certainly don't be ashamed.

We all have addictive personalities and therefore should not point the finger at people who have issues with alcohol, gambling, drugs etc. As a society, I firmly believe, we are collectively addicted to technology. This need to constantly have a phone in our hands, continuously finding out about other people and scrolling the net is simply not healthy.

We form these addictions at an early age and while technology is important and useful to all of us, when it is abused or overused it can be debilitating and even dangerous (scamming, fraud, cyber-bullying, catfishing, online stalking). To top it all, there are smart watches which keep you up to date every second of the day and night. They tell you how you slept, how many steps you took, what food and drink you consumed, whether it was good or bad for you... and you wonder why you have stress! The irony is they call this progress.

We need to stop looking at other people and judging them on their addictions. Instead, we should look at and admit to our own addictions. What's yours? Gossip, smoking, sex, coffee, tea, exercise, technology or storing things you don't need or use?

I remember working with Jo Scott in London when she was teaching me about Dr. Max Lüscher's colour therapy test. She told me I had to waste everything. Thirty-five years ago this concept was alien to me. I was brought up never to waste anything. A few months ago, though, I thought about this concept and understood it – a lightbulb moment!

Let go of everything you don't need or use. Like negative thoughts in your head, useless clutter in your home is only taking up space that could be better used, and unburdening yourself will make you feel so much better.

We also need to stop thinking that one addiction is worse than another. That someone addicted to drugs is more at risk than someone with a gambling or alcohol problem. This is simply not the case. We must own our addictions and do something about them in order to live by example and contribute healthily to the world as a whole.

We are the micro in the macro. If we can manage our addictions and maybe even help others do the same, we can change the quality of the world in general. We must remind ourselves that when we judge others, we are judging ourselves.

We are our own judge, jury and executioner. We can only avoid a long sentence of self-loathing and guilt if we can acknowledge our addiction and make the first tiny steps towards overcoming it.

Let me share a wonderful holistic therapy technique that has been proven to help people with addictive personalities to shift their focus and resist temptation. The Emotional Freedom Technique (EFT) is an alternative treatment for physical pain and emotional distress. It's also referred to as tapping or psychological acupressure.

People who use this technique believe tapping the body can create a balance in your energy system and treat pain. According to its developer, Gary Craig, a disruption in energy is the cause of all negative emotions and pain.

Tapping is a great way of identifying and owning your addictions. Combined with a specific deep breathing technique to release stress, tapping can transport us into the inner calm part of our minds. It is very simple to do and involves finding the acupressure points on your body. We have many pressure points on our body, so you can mix it up a bit when practising this technique. For me, the most effective area is my forehead and chest. For now, just remembering a few of these points and practising regularly is the best way forward for you.

5-minute tapping exercise

Stop wherever you are and take a deep breath in. Then let it out and begin tapping with your fingertips on the fatty area beneath your pinky finger (don't stop). As you do, notice how you're feeling (anxious, depressed, etc.). Sit with it for a moment.

And then, while still tapping:

1. Identify the issue. What is the distress is about? Name it. This will be your focus for the exercise. (Continue tapping.)

2. Rate the intensity. How strong is it on a scale from 1 to 10? 10 being the most intense. (Tap on.)

3. While still tapping, notice what you're feeling in your body; be present to it. Then think of a comforting phrase like, "Even though I'm feeling all this anxiety, I choose to relax and feel safe now." Do that two more times while still tapping.

4. Tap each of the following points on your body eight times consecutively (like you're sending Morse Code), repeating the comforting phrase three times as you do. Continue tapping and reciting while you work your way down your body.

a. First, the eyebrow.

b. Next, the side of the eye.

c. Then, under the eye.

d. And, under the nose.

> e. Next, the chin.
>
> f. Then, the top of the collarbone.
>
> g. And under the arm (or armpit).
>
> h. End at the top of the head.
>
> Repeat the sequence. This time, notice how your anxiety is lessening and fading away. Notice feelings of safety and calm growing in your body. End after three times through.
>
> 5. Rate the intensity. How strong is your anxiety now on a scale of 1 to 10? (Repeat as necessary.)

Like all exercises, tapping takes time to get right and feel the effects. It's certainly not a quick fix. It's not a case of a few wee taps and suddenly all addictions or temptations are gone.

All I ask is that you make tapping part of your daily routine and be open to the power this technique can have. You don't even need to stop what you are doing to do it. You can sit at your computer and just take a moment to breathe, let go of tension and tap. If your eyes are getting tired as you work, just close them, rest for a moment and tap on your preferred points.

As you sit there tapping your shoulders, arms, and your spine, be aware of your posture – is it also draining your energy? Be aware of what's on the computer and the position of the computer. Are these causing too much stress? Is it time for a break?

Remind yourself as often as you need that a computer is only a machine. You have to program it in order that it may give you back information. You control it, it should not control you.

The accompanying breath required during tapping is not the involuntarily breathing of our respiratory system. It is the deliberate, voluntary impulse to pause and be aware of your breathing, its depth, its pace and its effect on the body and mind.

If you work in a room with a window. Look out of the window and find something natural to focus on – a leaf, the sky, the effects of a breeze. Focussing on something that is the opposite to a machine really helps you to temporarily disconnect from it.

My favourite place to practise tapping and breathing is by the window of my Donegal home as I look out at the sea. I breathe in as the waves come in, then pause for a second before releasing the breath as the waves break and pull back from the shore. We can learn from nature to observe the breath, imagining that the in-breath is bringing a wonderful life-force in and after a short pause, the out-breath is letting go of all stress. I was a poor sleeper in the past, and now if I wake in the middle of the night, all I need to do is tap, tap, tap and then I sleep, sleep, sleep.

Take yourself outside for a walk as soon as you can and treat yourself to the soothing effect this wonderful technique can have.

CHAPTER TEN

People are always going to hurt you, choose the ones who are worth suffering for.

As I have mentioned many times, I firmly believe in a collective consciousness. I believe we are always picking up on each other's thoughts. Therefore, as we approach the end of this book, I compel you to choose the right people to have around you as you continue to explore your self-healing journey.

Where possible, surround yourself with strong, gentle, compassionate, wise people.

I believe that people come into your life for a reason, a season, or a lifetime.

When someone is in your life for a reason, it is usually to meet a need you have expressed. They have come to assist you through a difficult time, to provide you with guidance and support, to aid you mentally, physically, emotionally, or spiritually. They are a godsend. They are there for the reason that you need them for. Then, without any wrongdoing on anyone's part, the relationship ends. Sometimes they die, sometimes they just drift away. What we must realise is that our need has been met and their work is done. The prayer you sent has been answered and now it is time for you take the lesson and move on.

Some people come into your life for a season, because it's your time to share, grow or learn. They bring you an experience of peace or make you laugh. They may teach you something you have never done. They can give you an abundance of joy. Believe it, it is real, yet only for a season. This reminds me of the season in the 80s when I did all the courses. The people I met, both students and teachers, helped me to some degree at that time, even though they were not destined to be in my life forever.

Lifetime relationships teach lifetime lessons; things you must build upon in order to a have a solid emotional foundation. Your part is to accept the learning, love the person, and put what you have learned to use in all other relationships and areas of your life. It is said that love is blind, yet friendship is clairvoyant. True friends have a sixth sense ability to know how to advise, support or just be with you.

> Now take a moment to think about those people who have come into your life for a reason, a season and a lifetime, and give thanks for them.

Sadly, one thing you can be sure of, even those people who love you, will hurt you. Even family, friends and colleagues can and will disappoint or hurt you at some point. So, make sure when you are choosing 'your people' that they are the ones who are worth suffering for.

Think about who you have already chosen throughout your life and recall those times when they did hurt or let you down. Have you taken on their issues? Is it time to give them back?

Now remind yourself all the reasons why this person is worth suffering for. Remind yourself that, like you, they are only human.

I would encourage you to deal with this hurt and move past it in the healthiest of ways. You can deal with the hurt and maintain a closeness with the person by writing a letter to them.

First ask yourself, why you allow them to hurt you.

Then list all the hurts. Number them 1-10, with 10 being the deepest.

Now write the following letter to the person, filling in the gaps.

I choose not to carry _____ around with me anymore. I am letting you go. I am freeing myself from your power over me. I choose not to take on your issues, so they stay with you. They are not mine.

CONCLUSION

We live in our minds so choose strong, positive thoughts. Everyday tell yourself, "I am beautiful because I exist not for what I do or say. I am beautiful in every way. I love and approve of myself now, for now is the only time I have."

By way of drawing our time together to an end, please join me now in writing one of the most important letters you may ever write, a letter to yourself.

In it, forgive yourself any wrongdoings in your past. Acknowledge any proud moments in your past and present. List your strengths and your passions. List your hopes and dreams. And now for the crucial part. Describe the person you are going to work towards being, making sure you give yourself credit for how far you have come already in the course of reading this book.

No one is going to see this letter so don't let that beast called fear stop you from saying everything you need to. Think of this as a way to reflect back in order to move forward. There are no restrictions on how much or how little you write. There are no right or wrong words. And it certainly doesn't matter about the spelling! This is not going on Facebook,

> Twitter or Instagram. This is going into a safe place that only you know about. Once you have written it, put it away. Then, in times when you are plateauing, spiralling or just feel stuck, read the letter to remind yourself how strong and confident you have been and can be again.

Through my life, especially during periods of deep-rooted change, I was fascinated by examining what therapists referred to as my *Web of Life,* which I likened to the pattern on our sails in Chapter One. We all have a sail and yours, like mine, will be made up of all those who have influenced you throughout life; family, friends, neighbours, relatives, teachers, doctors, ministers, priests, nuns, staff, colleagues. Your sail's intricate pattern will be made up of the experiences, the places and events that have moulded you into the person you are today. Your thoughts, feelings, actions, creations and movements will also have made their own unique design on the sail. The people you have met on your journey and those you have never met, yet have been inspired by, will have helped to decorate and strengthen your sail.

Think about your sail and especially the people that have made a mark on it for one reason or another. The person you have become is because of these people, places and things. And not just the positive ones, the negative ones too. The negative people or experiences will have taught you more about yourself than you may think, and helped mould you into the person you are today. I call negative people my *friendly enemies*.

Think about what type of person you are today. Write it down. Now be brave and write down how you used to describe yourself to others. Write down how you used to see yourself. No one else is going to read this so be brutally honest. Then write down how you hope to describe yourself to others having embarked on your self-healing journey with the help of this book.

Being brutally honest, I used to be a fraud and a jealous, frightened, insecure person. Today I am a confident, genuine person. I enjoy my own company. I am a person who can face up to fear. I am a person who can delight in the little things. I am a person who lives in the moment. I am a person who can cope with whatever life throws at me.

I would seriously go out and skip up and down the streets of Cookstown if that's what I felt like doing. If it would bring me joy in that given moment, I would do it. I do not second guess or concern myself with what people think about me anymore.

70% of the time I like myself and 90% of the time I love myself. I'm still not better than anyone else, I'm just equal. Compared to someone with billions or nothing at all, I'm still equal to them. They are part of me and I'm part of them.

You cannot travel this journey alone. We are not islands. We need other people around us to create the energy to make us grow and develop into the best person we can be.

One light will shine into the darkness, yet many lights will lead the way out of the darkness. If you participate in your own healing the darkness will not cover you completely and the roaring of the thunder will not harm you. The wind will push you in different directions, my friends, and that is when you need to adjust your sail.

I hope my book has taught you how to do exactly that.

Today I am happy, healthy, successful and peaceful.

Let me finish with this story.

I was in the company of my very bright grandson Thomas a few years ago when he observed me swimming, something I love to do. Afterwards, he boasted that his sister Imogen was like the **sailfish** *when she swam. Little did I know the sailfish is the fastest fish in the ocean, reaching speeds of 68 miles per hour. Their large size and spirited fight make them a favourite among trophy fishers too. Once my grandson had educated me on this creature, he went on to describe me as a* **snailfish**, *the slowest swimmer in the world. Granted, I knew there was no such thing, yet his words that day have inspired me.*

Regardless of the size of your boat or your sail, despite the speed you journey through life, or whether you are the largest trophy fish in the ocean or the tiniest known to mankind, you have a unique and vital part to play in this world. You have a purpose for your time on earth that is just as important as anyone else's.

You have it in you to sail onwards and upwards towards self-love and acceptance. Just remember, keep your head up and enjoy the view from the top of every wave as much as the peace and calm of still waters.

SHEILA'S SAYINGS

I am enough.

I am beautiful because I exist not because of what I do or say.

I AM Beautiful.

You will never have enough of what you don't need.

We are our emotions.

It's none of your business what other people think of you.

I love and approve of myself, unconditionally.

Love yourself for who you are and not what other people expect you to be.

You expend too much energy trying to make people like you.

Happiness is the highest form of health.

Today I am happy, healthy, successful and peaceful.

I love myself always.

People are always going to hurt you, choose the ones who are worth suffering for.

Change your thoughts, change your mind.

Meditation is not something you need try hard to do. It is simply being in the NOW.

Breathe, breathe, breathe.

Healer, heal thyself.

Breath is life and life is breath.

Now is all we have.

Thought is the first process of action.

Never assume as you will only make an ASS out of U and ME.

I can only heal myself.

Think it, feel it, do it!

If you don't love yourself, you haven't the capacity to love others.

You have the power within you to create great things. Use it wisely.

Always listen to your gut, this is your third brain.

Listen to the words that others speak for there is wisdom and healing within.

Fear knocked on the door. Courage answered. There was no one there.

Live in the NOW, forever.

Everything is energy.

Trust that we never walk alone.

The darkness will not cover me completely.

I choose love, light and peace always.

The things you do not like in others are the things you do not like in yourself.

I am content in my own skin.

DADDY'S SAYINGS

(Words of Wisdom from Gerry Conway)

It won't always be dark at half past four.

It's like the flies (Why do flies go up the chimney? Because it soots them!).

I am in business to do myself good, not to do anyone harm.

It's like Eamon Andrews (This Is Your Life).

If you take a risk you might fail, if you don't take a risk, you are sure to fail.

It took a man forty years to learn patience.

If you want a job done, ask a busy man.

Only be as honest as the person you are dealing with.

Never start an argument unless you are going to win it.

ACKNOWLEDGEMENT

Thanks to Audrey & Philip.

Audrey, without you ghost writing my words and experiences, these two books might never have have happened. I can't thank you enough for the excellent job you did.

Phil, thank you for putting my books together. Your expertise in self-publishing, design and computer skills are A*. Not to mention your patience with this technology dinosaur!

May you both fly high with the wind on your backs, hoisting your sails into writing and publishing books for all those like me, who had the life experiences and just needed some expertise and guidance to get them into print.

Love, light & abundance in all great things,

Sheila

Printed by Amazon Italia Logistica S.r.l.
Torrazza Piemonte (TO), Italy

47891713R00067